Learn How to
Blow Glass

Anne Kramer

Learn How to Blow Glass
by Anne Kramer

ISBN 978-0-9866426-0-9

Printed in the United States of America

Copyright © 2010 Psylon Press

The images on pages 30, 32, 42 and 46
© Getty Images

Latest books by Psylon Press:

100% Blonde Jokes
R. Cristi
ISBN 978-0-9866004-1-8

Choosing a Dog Breed Guide
Eric Nolah
ISBN 978-0-9866004-5-6

Best Pictures Of Paris
Christian Radulescu
ISBN 978-0-9866004-8-7

Best Gift Ideas For Women
Taylor Timms
ISBN 978-0-9866004-4-9

Contents

Introduction

Welcome to How to Learn Glass Blowing. As we will learn, glass blowing has a long and interesting history that dates back thousands of years. This unique guide will introduce you not only to the history of this interesting art form but will also take you through some of the most common glass blowing techniques as well as the steps that need to be understood to begin basic glass blowing.

While hands-on instruction in a reputable glass blowing studio is always recommended, this guide will present you with all of the information you need to get started, including the types of equipment and supplies you will need to embark on this exciting journey.

Let's get started!

A History of Glassmaking

- 1700 B.C. Glass manufacturing is established in Syria

- 2450 B.C. An excavation of a Mesopotamian Cemetery unearths a great many glass beads.

- 1450 B.C. Egyptians create beautiful glass vases with a sand armature. Trails of hot glass are wrapped around a "sand core" that determines the shape of the vessel.

- 1200 B.C. Techniques for casting hot glass into molds are created.

- 100 B.C. Glass blowing is first developed in Syria

- 50 B.C. Glass blowing techniques begin to flourish in Phoenicia.

- 680 A.D. Glassmakers arrive in Britain from Gaul (France)

- 1000 A.D. Venice begins to work with glass; it will soon establish itself as the glass center of the world.

- 1291 A.D. Venetian government orders the entire glass industry moved to the island of Murano to prevent outbreaks of fire in the city as well as to conceal the secrets of the Venetian glass works.

- 1600-France becomes established as a major power within the glass industry. Henry IV confers exclusive rights to certain Italians to produce glass within specified cities in France.

- 1608 A.D. The first glass factory is established in British colony of Jamestown.

- 1615 A.D. Coal furnaces are introduced in England after wood furnaces are banned.

- 1673 A.D. George Ravenscroft develops lead crystal; the British are no longer restricted by the expensive Venetian monopoly on glass.

- 1827 A.D. Deming Jarves establishes the Sandwich Glass Company in Cape Cod. He introduces a pressing machine that imitates cut glass for less.

- 1858 A.D. Heinrich Geissler and Julius Plucker create the predecessor of the neon sign, "Geissler tubes."

- 1858 A.D. The Mason jar is invented in New York

- 1868 A.D. Corning Glass Works produces light bulbs for Thomas Edison

- 1887 A.D. Glass making has transitioned from traditional mouth blowing to a semi-automatic process as Ashley introduces a machine that is capable of producing 200 bottles per hour in Yorkshire; more than three times faster than traditional methods.

- 1890 Louis Tiffany begins to use stained glass for art forms and lamps.

- 1897 A.D. The first semi-automatic glass bottle making machine is invented by Frank C. Ball.

- 1898 A.D. Sir William Ramsay and Morris William Travers discover the element neon

- 1900 A.D. Michael Owens invents an automatic glass blowing machine.

- 1923 A.D. The Gob feeder is invented

- 1960 A.D. the FDA gives glass the GRAS (Generally Recognized as Safe) rating. Glass is still the only packaging material to receive this designation.

Chapter 1

The Basics of Glassblowing

Before you can begin with the basics of actual glassblowing, it is important to first develop an understanding of the basic properties associated with glass so that you can have a better appreciation of how it is formed.

The Basic Properties of Glass

Like any other solid or even metal, glass does have a melting point. Many people are not aware of this but glass is actually no more than liquid that is in a hardened form. Even a glass of water is actually one type of liquid contained inside another liquid. These are all basics of any introductory chemistry class, but it becomes even more important when you are learning the basics involved in making glass and glassblowing.

Glass is formed from oxides. The most important of those oxides is sand. The other oxides make glass either softer or harder. For instances, soda oxide produces glass that is softer so you will need to use a lesser degree of heat in order to effectively work with it. Lime can make glass harder. In addition, oxides can also make many different colors. In its most natural form glass is actually a light green color but when small amounts of magnesium or nickel are added it is possible to make purple glass. If you want red glass, you need to use cadmium. Yellow glass is produced by adding silver oxides.

The hotter the temperature the softer the glass will become. This is one of the basic essential to glassblowing that must be understood as heat is the most critical element involved in glassblowing. One of the most common mistakes that many people make when first beginning glassblowing is in not understanding just how important heat is to glassblowing. As a result, they commonly do not use the proper amount of heat for the size of glass they are working with. If you are working with two pieces of glass it is also important for both pieces to have the same temperature.

It can be incredibly easy to overheat one piece and not apply the same amount of heat to the other piece. In order for the two pieces to be joined together they absolutely must have the same precise temperature. Failure to understand this critical concept will result in the production of weak joints; which means that eventually one piece will break away from the other. This problem is common referred to as a cold seal.

You must also use common sense in glassblowing as well in order to understand whether one piece is perhaps too hot or too cold. Timing can be critical in glassblowing. If you allow a piece of glass to heat too quickly, it can break.

As you can see, temperature and heating are essential to the art of glassblowing. We will refer back to these elements again in later sections as we begin to discuss the different techniques involved in glassblowing.

Types of Glass

It is also important to understand that there are two basic types of glass; hard glass and soft glass. Hard glass is also known as borosilicate glass. This type of glass is commonly sold in three different forms:

- Clear rods
- Clear tubing
- Colored rods

It should be kept in mind that these two different types of glasses cannot be adhered to one another.

The most common type of glass used in glassblowing is hard borosilicate glass. This is the same type of glass that is produced by the Corning Glass Company, more commonly known by consumers as Pyrex. It is produced by other manufacturing companies as well but most people still refer to it as Pyrex.

Colored glass can be used with this type of glass as well and can be easily purchased from lampworking suppliers. It is available in colored rods. Some of the most well known manufacturers for this type of glass include Zimmerman, Kugler, Gaffer and Reichenbach.

Glassblowing Equipment and Supplies

In order to get started with glassblowing you will need several pieces of equipment as well as some supplies. These are all tools that you will need to become familiar with as you become more involved with the art of glassblowing.

Kiln

The kiln is the tool that is used for melting your glass. It is a type of box that is heavily insulated and must be kept hot at all times to melt the raw chemicals that are used to make up the formula for glass. When you melt a new batch of chemicals, the kiln turns them to molten glass. You should be aware that the kiln, which is really a furnace, can reach 2000 degrees or even more.

Kilns may be heated with gas or electricity. A day furnace offers the advantage of being able to be heated the night before so that you can use it the following day. The disadvantage to this type of kiln is that it is expensive and as a result is usually only found in professional glassblowing studios.

A pot furnace is smaller in size and is also free-standing. The small size makes them ideal for a private workspace.

Glory Hole

The glory hole is a type of second furnace that is used for heating glass. You can turn it on and off as you need in order to reheat your glass throughout the process of glassblowing. Usually, the glory hole is a type of drum gas with forced air. If you have already seen the process of glassblowing you are probably familiar with the glory hole even though you may not have known what it was called. It is where a pipe with a piece of glass on the end is positioned for reheating.

Torch

As previously discussed, heat is essential to glassblowing. You cannot blow glass without heat. Once the molten glass has been removed from the kiln, the torch becomes critical for applying additional heat to the glass. The torch features an outer flame that makes it possible to work with more glass. There is also an inner flame for detail working. When you work with a torch in glassblowing it is also sometimes known as lampworking.

Yoke

The yoke is the place where the glassblower places the pipe when working. A ball bearing is attached to the yoke so that the glassblower will be able to rotate the pipe.

Punty

The punty is really just a pipe or a hollow rod which is usually either graphite or stainless steel and is used for transferring a piece from the blowpipe onto the pipe or punty. This makes it possible for the glassblower to open another section on the piece as well as for bringing in smaller amounts of glass from the furnace in order to add to the piece being worked on. In addition, it can be used for creating solid objects and even for adding decorating and handles to other pieces of glass. A punty can range in size and may be very small or even quite large in order to accommodate the size of the piece being created.

Pipewarmer

The piperwamer is used by the glassblower for warming the punties or pipes. Without warming the pipes, it is impossible for the glass to stick. The pipes absolutely must be sufficiently hot so that they have a glow that is red hot.

Blowpipe

The blowpipe is used by the glassblower for blowing a bubble of molten glass. Blowpipes are hollow and are usually about five feet in length, although the width could be as small as half an inch or as large as two inches. Hot glass can be picked up using the blowpipe.

Marver

A marver is a flat plate or surface that is rather heavy and fireproof. It is used for rolling, flattening and shaping molten glass. Normally, a marver will be made from graphite or steel and can be used for cooling and shaping the glass.

Blocks

Blocks are typically made from cherry wood because this type of wood has the highest tolerance for high temperatures. The blocks are used for cooling and shaping glass after the marver has been utilized. You will find there are different shaped blocks which can be used for different uses.

Jacks and Tweezers

Another indispensable tool to glassblowing is a set of tweezers, which allow you to move hot glass. Jacks work to shape the glass and are commonly used for making a neck on a glass bubble. They are also sometimes known as mashers.

Shears and Scissors

Scissors can be used for cutting the glass while it is still hot. Many lampworkers are now using Japanese bonsai shears for this purpose.

Nippers

A type of cutter, nippers can be used for snipping glass rods when they are cold.

Scoring Knife

This is another essential tool to glassblowing that is used for cutting tubing and rods. Carbide steel knives are popular because they will not become dull.

Water

When you work with heat in glassblowing it can be useful to have a bucket of water in which you can place hot tools to cool them off quickly. Do be sure you have dried off your tools after wetting them to avoid any cracking.

Annealing Oven

An annealing oven is a type of chamber that is used for gradually cooling down glass to room temperature in order to prevent it from cracking. It usually takes approximately 24 hours to adequately cool a piece of glass. When glass is properly annealed it will maintain the longevity of the piece.

Bench

A bench can be used for supporting the blow-pipes when they are rolled back and forth. It is usually made from wood or metal

Hot Pot

A hot pot is a metal container that is fireproof and is used for throwing scraps of hot glass into.

Ventilation Equipment

There are many different types of appliances on the market including attic fans and hoods that can be used for exhausting the fumes that can be created from the combustion process; resulting in high levels of carbon monoxide. You should never proceed with glassblowing unless you have proper ventilation.

Using Your Tools Together

That is certainly a lot of equipment and you are probably wondering how all of the different pieces are used and in what order they should be used. Here is an overview of the basic process:

The kiln is used for turning the glass into molten glass. The tip of the blowpipe will be preheated and then dipped into the molten glass to pick it up. At this point it is said that the molten glass has been gathered or collected onto the tip of the molten glass has been gathered or collected onto the tip of the blowpipe. This may take several dips.

Next, the marver will be used in order to roll the glass for shaping. A thin crust will be formed on the outside. You will then blow into the pipe in order to form a bubble. If you are trying to make a larger piece you will need to gather more molten glass once again from the kiln and add it at this point.

Blocks will be used for further shaping and cooling of the glass that has been gathered. Shears can also be utilized for making linear cuts as well as for snipping off larger pieces of glass. Once the piece has reached a further stage of completion, jacks are used as well as tweezers for pulling parts of the glass and detail work.

After the piece has reached the shape and size that is desired, the bottom will be completed first and then the piece will be moved to the punty so that the top can be finished.

Staying Safe

Anytime you are working with potentially toxic fumes and extreme levels of heat, it is always critical to take safety precautions. Be sure you avoid any flammable situations within the home and instead work in the garage or a similar area. Never work on a surface that is not fireproof.

You can also help to reduce flammable combustion by checking where you are working as well as any chemicals that may be nearby. Be aware of any motors or portable heaters that may be nearby and which could produce sparks or flames. You should also take note of the air flow within the workspace and be sure there are now down drafts that could potentially push fire or hazardous flames from the torch.

Of course, you should also make sure that you always have adequate ventilation within your workspace. Some people choose to use a fan so that the ventilation will be directed out a window. It is crucial to always have an exhaust fan and an open window when glassblowing. All vapors and gasses should be drawn away from you.

If you are involved in lampworking and using propane, be sure to pipe the propane in from the outdoors and never use any bottled propane indoors. The importance of using outdoor tanks cannot be stressed enough.

More importantly, take care that any gas tanks are secured to a wall or some other type of secure surface in order to prevent the regulator from breaking off or the tanks from falling over. If the regulator should fall off it will cause the gas to escape far faster and can result in the canister becoming extremely dangerous.

Always be sure you have a fire extinguisher nearby along with a first aid kit in the event of an accident. If you have long hair, make sure it is tied back. Never wear loose sleeves or any other type of loose clothing while glassblowing.

In addition, you will need to wear protective eyewear. The best type of protective eyewear is the type made from didymium to filter out the yellow glare that comes from working with flame and hot glass. Exposure to this glass over the long term can cause serious harm to your eyes. Welder's glasses are tinted so dark that it can be difficult to work with them.

Chapter 2

Glassblowing Principles

There is often a certain sense of mystery associated with the art of glassblowing but in reality it is actually a fairly simple process. In fact, it is not that much different from blowing a bubble using a straw. The only real difference lies in the materials you are using. In the case of glassblowing you are using molten hot materials. Globs of molten glass are collected from the oven onto the end of the pipe and you then blow through the pipe to form a bubble in the glass at the end of the pipe.

The glass will need to be rotated frequently and then cooled and reheated so that you can shape it to the rough dimensions that are desired for the final piece. The real art involved in glassblowing comes in when you begin to pull, rotate and shape the glass on the marver as well as when you add in color. Rotation is essential to glassblowing because this is what actually determines the way in which the molten glass will react.

If the glass is rotated too slowly it can droop, but if you hold the glass on the tip of the pip too high you will not be able to gain the form that you desire in most cases. It is also imperative that you ensure the pipe or rod is kept horizontal.

The first thing that you will need to do in order to get started with glassblowing is to make sure that you have the kiln or furnace going as well as the secondary furnace; the glory hole.

Remember, the glory hole is the furnace that will be used for reheating your piece of glass while you are still working on it.

As you get started, you will preheat the tip of the blowpipe and then dip it into the molten glass which is inside the furnace. This step is known as gathering because you are gathering the glass onto the end of the pipe. When you are actually doing this you may note that it is much like using a spoon to gather honey from within a jar. In fact, you may even find that this is a good way to practice gathering molten glass because it will give you a good hands-on feeling for the way that gravity can impact substances that are semi-liquid, such as honey or molten glass.

In order to achieve a fair sized bubble that you can blow, you will most likely need to gather the glass several times by dipping the pipe in and out. Once the molten glass has been gather to the desired size on t he end of the blowpipe you will then need to roll it out on the marver. The marver will help to form a skin on the outside of the bubble that is cooling while also helping in shaping it.

Be sure that the glass is kept near the edge of the marver surface while you are working on it. Be aware that it could eel as though it is going to fall but unless you roll it off the edge it shouldn't. Continue rotating and before long you should see the bubble begin to take shape. You will need to focus on keeping the pipe horizontal and con-

tinue rotating at this stage.

You should also begin to see that the sides of the piece will start to even up. Once this has occurred, you will need to tilt the rod upward so that you can achieve a shape that is more oval. It may take some practice to get this part right, so have patience.

Be aware that it is critical to ensure your movements remain fluid while you continually rotate the piece in order to achieve the correct outcome. Do not be surprised if you are not satisfied with the way the piece looks the first few times you try this. It does take practice. If you do not like the way it looks, you can always reheat it using the glory hole or just start over from the beginning with a new gathering of molten glass and start a new bubble.

If you do like the way the piece is starting to take shape, you can then gather more molten glass if you would like to make the piece larger. Blocks can be used for cooling pieces during the early stages. They are helpful for holding basic shapes of glass.

At this point, you can then introduce the glass-blowing tools and start pulling and shaping the glass. The bench will be critical at this stage because you can use it for holding tools while you are working on the piece. The tools that you decide to use will depend on the piece that you are working on and what you desire to make. For instance, if you are forming a flat bottom for a vase or something similar then you would need to use paddles. On the other hand, if you are forming a bubble to start the opening of a piece, then the tweezers would be best. Tweezers and paddles are both available in graphite for working with hot glass.

If you would like to add color to your piece you can bring in solid colored glass rods. It will need to be lampworked until it is pliable. This is something that we will cover in greater detail in another section.

As you can see, while the art of glassblowing sounds complicated and difficult, the basic process is really fairly straightforward and simple.

Chapter 3

Making your First Piece

In the proceeding chapter we discussed how to get started making a bubble. The next step is to work toward making an actual piece such as a vase, bowl or tumbler; all of which can be started from a bubble.

Step 1. Blow the beginning bubble

Step 2. Gather additional molten glass on the bubble. Remember that it may take several gatherings in order to have enough glass for the piece you need, so continue dipping the pipe into the glory hole. If your plan is to make a bowl or a tumbler you will certainly need to gather more glass onto the pipe. Make certain the entire bubble is completely coated with glass and continue turning the pipe so that you have an even coating.

Step 3. Now you are going to proceed with blocking. As previously mentioned a block is really a type of mold, usually made of cherry wood that can be used to place your gathering onto. It helps to provide the symmetry for the piece you are creating. Blocks are available in a variety of different sizes so make sure you choose the size that is most appropriate for the piece you are working on.

The block will also make it possible for you to rotate the molten glass and cool the exterior skin.

You should not expect to see a precise glass object at this stage of the process. At this point, you goal is to aim for symmetry. The final shape will not be achieved until you begin using the marver and hand tools at a later stage of the project.

Step 4. Now you are going to begin working on shaping the piece. You will most likely need to blow the glass again at this point. If it has cooled too much you will need to use the glory hole to reheat it. Try to only reheat the portions that have cooled rather than the entire piece. Once you have the desired consistency, you can then blow the glass until it has achieved the desired thickness. Once the walls of the piece have the desired thickness, you are then ready to move on to the marver.

Step 5. As previously discussed, the marver is a flat surface that is fireproof and is used for shaping hot glass. You can find marvers in a variety of different sizes, including those that are as large as tables. Choose the size that is most appropriate for the piece you are working on and drop the glob of glass onto the marver. Do not be surprised if the piece looks something like a droopy piece of dough. That is fine. That is what it is supposed to look like at this point.

Begin moving the marver from one side to the other so that the mound of glass will roll back and forth. The goal at this point is to make the glob of glass look cylindrical. Over time the shape will become more defined as the cool surface of the

marver stiffens the exterior of the glass. Keep in mind that it does take practice to master marvering just like it takes practice to make bubbles.

You can also shape the molten glass using your hands and a piece of wet newspaper. This method is very similar to using a block, with the exception that the piece can be more easily bent and shaped. Hot gas will form between the newspaper and the glass so that it is easier to turn the hot piece. Keep in mind that you will most likely need to rewet the newspaper from time to time so that you do not get burned while you are shaping the piece.

One problem that you may encounter while you are working on the piece is that it could become too bottom heavy. If that happens, the best thing to do is to angle the pipe up. Gravity plays an important role in glassblowing and you can use it to your advantage to gain the shape that you desire while you are marvering. Continually adjusting the angle of the marver will allow you to create the walls of the piece you are creating, whether it is a bowl, vase or tumbler. Keep in mind as well that you can also blow more air into the piece to define its shape and size even further.

Creating a Neck

When you are ready to create an opening in the piece, such as for a bowl or a vase you will need to have the jacks ready. The jacks are the tools that will be primarily used for creating openings. They are similar to large tweezers. Remember that you will need to reheat the glass in the glory hole prior to jacking the neck of the glass. Once you have reheated the glass, take the jacks and squeeze them at the end of the bubble.

Remember that you will need to continue to rotate the pipe even while you are necking or jacking the piece using the jacks. The rotation of the pipe will ensure the piece remains centered and this is essential. You certainly do not want your piece to topple over once it is finished.

In addition, remember to use care when applying the jacks. Use them gently or you could very easily break the neck of the glass by applying too much pressure. You may well need to use several attempts in order to determine the correct amount of pressure to apply. This is something you will learn through time and practice.

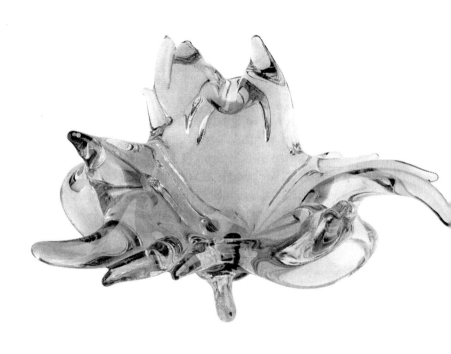

Creating the Bottom

When you are ready to create the bottom of the piece you will need to go back to the glory hole to reheat it but try to do so only at the bottom. In order to flatten the bottom of the piece so that it will actually form a stable base you will need to use the paddles to press gently on the bottom of the piece. Remember; gently. Do not press hard or the piece will cave in. In addition, as you work on the bottom of the piece, remember that the base will generally be thicker than the sides so try to avoid making it too flimsy or thin.

The next step is to remove the piece from the blowpipe so you will need to have the punty ready at this stage. The punty, you may recall, is the rod that you will use for moving pieces of hot glass. It can also be used in later stages for decorating using small pieces of hot glass. There are punties available in all different sizes, so be sure that you choose the punty that is most appropriate for the piece you are creating. The diameter of the punty must be wide enough to allow you to handle the piece securely.

Once you have reheated the bottom using the glory hole so that it is soft enough, be sure that the punty is centered in the middle of the piece. Remember; allow gravity to work for you; not against you.

Now, you are going to take everything to your handy bucket of water and cool off the neck on your piece. The water will work to harden the neck and create a point where you can break the piece off the blowpipe. You can lightly knock on the pipe and the glass should break away from it. Take the glass, which should remain attached to the punty and insert it in the glory hole to reheat it once again. Keep in mind that speed is essential. Every part of the piece will need to be reheated, but the most important part is the neck because it must remain sufficiently pliable so that it can be opened up. Regardless of whether you are making a vase, a tumbler or a bowl, all your piece will need is an opening.

Okay, now you are ready to turn your piece into your final vision. Grab the jacks and insert them into the neck of your piece. Use only the tips of the jacks to focus on the neck. Use one hand to turn the punty as you insert the jacks into the neck with the other hand at the same time. Open up the lips of the neck gradually until you have achieved the desired size.

If your goal is to obtain a tumbler with straight edges, you will need to keep the jacks parallel with one another. If you want a wider mouth for your tumbler, you should angle the jacks in an upward manner. The angle that you hold the jacks is extremely important. So important, in fact, that it will actually determine what you create and whether it is a vase or a tumbler or a bowl so pay careful attention to this stage.

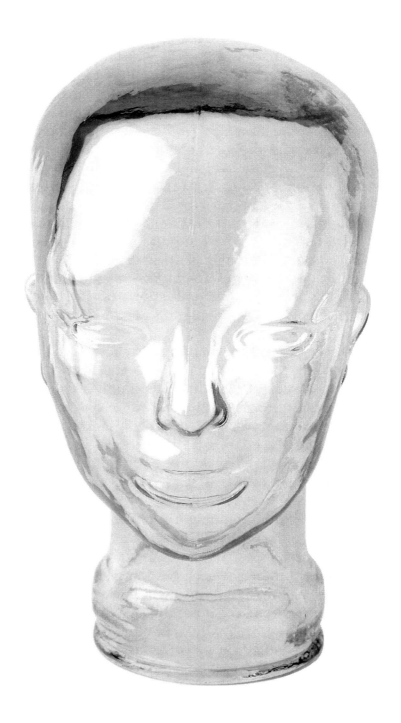

If you would like to make a bowl you are going to use precisely the same technique but you will leave more glass toward the base and open up the neck more. If you would like to make a bowl, simply repeat all of these steps, except create two necks. One neck will be positioned further down from the opening and another will be situated where you would insert the flowers. You should create the lower neck first. Reheat the piece and then form the second opening toward the top. Make the transfer in the same way you would do if you are creating a tumbler.

At this point you will need to prepare the piece to remove it from the punty. You will do this by tapping the punty. You can use any small utensil for doing this. Rotate the punty as you tap it. Be sure to wear fireproof gloves while you do this because next you are going to carry the piece of the annealing kiln.

As previously discussed, placing the piece into the annealing kiln will allow you to gradually cool it. The gradual cooling process makes it possible for the piece to achieve the necessary sturdiness and prevent any cracks from forming. Based on the size of the piece you are creating, you can expect for the annealing process to take from 12 to 24 hours. If you are creating something small like a bead, it won't take much time at all. Make sure you do not rush this process. Everything you have worked for up to this point will be for nothing if you rush it so have patience.

Adding Decorative Pieces or Handles

If you would like to add handles or any further decorative pieces, you will get started by gathering up more molten glass on the punty. Make sure you continue to turn the rod so that the small piece of glass does not accidentally fall off. Remember, you will not need a lot. You may even find it helpful to have someone nearby to assist you at this stage.

Take the molten glass to the person helping you and have them grab the punty using graphite scissors or shears. The molten glass can then be quickly applied to the piece.

If you are going to attach a handle or handles to the piece, you use the same exact technique. The only difference is that the hot glass that is first attached and then pulled up to the spot where you want the other end of the handle to be positioned on the piece. Remember that a handle has two junctures. You can use the shears to remove the remaining additional glass. Use the tweezers as quickly as possible to be sure that the ends of the handle are secure. Turn the punty slowly while it remains attached to the glass.

Preheat the piece with the handle using the glory hole. As you remove it, you can also add any other finishing touches using the tweezers. Do not forget that the handle and the piece must be at the same temperature in order to prevent a cold seal from occurring, which can ultimately result in the handle falling off.

Chapter 4

Making Glass Beads

One of the most ancient art form is bead making. It is also closely associated with glassblowing. Although in the early days of bead making, artists tended to keep their techniques secret, today it is as simple as using a torch and using lampworking to create a bead. It may sound somewhat complicated but all that is really involved in bead making is using an extremely hot rod and placing hot molten glass on the tip. You then rotate the rod until you obtain the desired size and shape.

The only real difference between making any other type of glass and making a glass bead is the type of glass that is used. In almost all other forms of glassblowing hard glass is used. That is not the case with bead making. Beads must be made using soft glass, also sometimes known as soda lime glass. It is ideal for bead making because it has a lower melting point and is easier to work with. It is available in many different colors, just like hard glass; which can be beneficial when making beads.

Equipment Needed for Bead Making

Before we actually move on to discuss the techniques that are used for bead making, it is important to first discuss the tools and equipment you will need for this art. Many of the tools that you will need are the same as for any other form of glassblowing and include:

- An oxygen prone or propane torch
- A bench or stand to rest the torch in
- Annealing kiln
- Marver
- Tweezers
- Pliers

Along with this equipment, you will also need the following:

Mandrel

This is a stainless steel rod that is used for holding hot glass. It can also be used for forming holes in glass beads. The handle of the mandrel is rather then, making it easier to rotate quicker.

Bead Rake

This is a metal tool with a hook that can be used for making designs on beans

Tungsten Pick

This is a pick that is used for forming holes in the glass. It is heat resistant.

Optic Molds

These are used for making beads into various shapes.

Bead Reamers

This is used for cleaning the hole of the bead out once you are finished creating it.

Tile Nippers

These are used for cutting the glass.

Bead Release Separator

This is a thick type of liquid coating that can be used for preventing glass from sticking to metal. You can use it to coat the mandrel to make it easier to remove the glass from it once it has cooled.

Frit Powders

This is basically just colored glass that has been crushed. It can be used to add color to the beads you make. It is somewhat like sand in terms of consistency.

Dichroic Glass

This is a type of glass that can be placed on the surface of glass beads to make them reflect light and shimmer.

Stringers

These are thin strips of colored glass that can be used for decorating the outside of beads.

Copper Tubing

This is used to form a decorative base for beads. A small amount of it can be placed on the mandrel and then glass can be applied over it.

Safety Precautions in Bead Making

The same safety precautions that are used in regular glassblowing should be used when making beads. For instance, you should wear didymium glasses as well as work in an area that is fireproof. In addition, you should wear fireproof gloves and ensure you have good ventilation where you are working.

Making a Bead

To start making a bead, you will need to take the mandrel and dip it into the bead release separator. Next you need to heat the mandrel using the torch. Be sure that you have a safe place where you can lay it down while you are working. As the mandrel becomes red hot you will need to slightly move it away from the torch and then begin heating the glass.

Now, move the rod back and forth over the flame. Make sure you continue rotating the rod so that the glass will become molten. Remember that gravity can help you to keep the glass round and before long it will resemble a ball of honey.

After you have heated the glass rod, you will need to wind it around the mandrel that has been preheated, over the flame. Keep in mind that various colors of glass can do some strange things as they melt. For example, white can become transparent and red can turn black. Orange has a tendency to turn red.

Take the blob of molten glass to the tip of the mandrel and then pull the away the glass rod when a sufficient amount of the new bead is placed on the mandrel tip. Continue turning the bead around inside the flame. When you have reached the basic shape and size that you would like you will then remove the new molten bead from the flame. Next you are going to roll it over the marver until you achieve the desired shape.

Make sure you do not stop rolling the bead until the glass has stopped glowing.

If you would like to give the bead more of a tear shape, you will need to hold the mandrel up before it has dried. The molten glass will then droop downward and that will give you the tear shape. An annealing kiln will be necessary to properly dry the beads. It will take approximately 30 minutes in order for the beads to cool. Once a bead has cooled, you will need to utilize the mandrel with the pliers in order to twist the bead from the mandrel. Make sure you clean the bead as well as brush out the inside of the hole of the bead. You may find that soaking the bead in water at room temperature will help in removing any of the bead release substance that may remain.

If you would like to create other bead shapes, the next easiest option is an oblong bead. After the round blob of molten glass has turned red, you should allow it to cool down slightly until it has reached a dull orange in color. You can then roll it out on the marver like you are rolling out dough. You can also use a graphite paddle to even up the ends.

Adding Color to Beads

Stacking one color glass at a time with the use of the mandrel is by far the easiest way in which to add colors to beads. The key is to make sure the first color has slightly cooled before you attempt to add the second color. This technique will allow you to have two completely separate mounds that can then be rotated upon the marver for smoothness.

Once you have selected the color you would like to use you might also consider decorating it with some crushed colored glass, also known as frit. You can obtain frit in small packages of individual colors. It is usually sold at bead making stores. Frit should only be added while the bead is molten. Start by sprinkling the color frit you have chosen onto the marver and then roll the surface of the heated beat in the mixture of frit. The frit will begin to melt due to the heat of the bead.

Cane Making

This is another wonderful aspect of bead making. There are actually two different types of cane. One is more decorative and is used for decorating the exterior of a bead. These forms of cane are referred to as millefiore and murrini. Latticinio cane resembles a striped candy cane. The simple ribbon is the easiest form to learn if you are new to the process.

To get started creating a simple ribbon cane you will need to have several rods of different colors so that the ribbons will contrast with one another. Keep in mind that the rods should all be the same diameter so that you can achieve the best results. You will also need two rods of filigrana, which are rods that have opaque cores that have been subsequently covered with clear glass. In addition, you will need a contrasting opaque rod, which will be placed between the two filigranas.

To get started, heat one of the filigranas on one side until it is glowing. Then use a graphite marver to flatten it. Now, place it to the side and then repeat the process with the other filigrana, but instead of placing it to the side, hold it near the torch flame.

The next step is to heat the contrasting opaque rod. You will need to heat it until it has become very soft and then apply it to the other filigrana. Next, heat the first filigrana and then you are going to layer it on top of the two rod strips. Now, heat all three layers until they are all molten.

You will then begin to pull and twist the cane until you have created the ribbon effect. Once you are happy with the final result, go ahead and anneal it, slowly cooling it.

Chapter 5

Creating Glass Pipes

In the previous chapters we covered the basics of glass blowing. In this chapter we are going to take a look at the process that is used for creating glass pipes. The process of creating hand blown glass pipes is somewhat new and has actually become one of the more common types of glass blowing today. There are many different forms, shapes and varieties of glass pipes ranging from very simple to extremely elaborate. A glass pipe can be a single color or it can be a wide array of different colors. You should be aware that it does cost more money to make glass pipes but for most people they are well worth the cost as it makes it possible to combine self-expression with a high degree of artistry.

Many smokers do actually prefer a glass blown pipe over other options such as clay or metal. The glass does not add any flavor to the tobacco, which can be an advantage for the smoker who is a purist and who only wants to taste the tobacco. This is probably one of the main reasons why glass pipes have become so popular today.

There are also aesthetic reasons that have caused glass pipes to become so popular, including the contrasting patterns and colors that can be achieved. In addition, many people find there are other practical reasons associated with using a glass pipe, including the fact that when the pipe has a small hole drilled on the side it is possible to inhale on a more continuous basis.

Equipment Needed

Most of the equipment discussed in previous sections will also be needed for making glass pipes. Glass pipe making is a specialized type of glass blowing, so there are also a few other items that will be required.

Torches

There are many different types of torches on the market today but as a result of the special demands required of glass pipe making, the best type of torch to use is known as the Carlisle CC. This type of torch will produce a large flame but also makes it possible create finer details as well. You should know that it is one of the more expensive types of torches and costs around $1,000 but if you are planning on going into business for yourself and you are an advanced glass blower, you may find it to be well worth the cost.

If you are just starting out and/or you are not planning to go into business, then a regular torch that can be purchased for under $100 will suffice.

You will also need the following equipment:

- Graphite paddle
- Graphite marvering pad
- Tubing
- Oxygen
- Propane regulators and tanks
- Reamer
- Bowl pusher
- Hotfingers
- Glass
- Glass coloring materials

Both propane and oxygen can be obtained from a welding supply as well as other commercial suppliers. Keep in mind that both must be handled with the utmost care. Remember that the regulator must not be knocked off. Canisters should be chained firmly to another object so they cannot be knocked over. In addition, it is a good idea to make sure your canister is kept in a location that is not highly trafficked.

Along with the items listed above, you should also have a kiln for pipe making. While it is technically possible to create a pipe without using a kiln, if you want to make any type of advanced pipe you will definitely need a kiln, especially if you are going into business. The temperatures that can be achieved in a kiln will help to prevent your pipes from becoming brittle and being subject to breaking. Without these temperatures it is possible for the glass pipe to be vulnerable, which means that it could break during smoking and that is something you certainly do not want to happen. Through the use of a kiln, the stress in the worked glass can be eliminated, providing an annealing effect.

As for the actual glass itself, most people prefer to use borosilicate, or hard glass. This type of glass is obviously harder, which is better for making a pipe and it is also more compatible with other types of glass that you might want to affix to the pipe.

Remember that you should also have a good ventilation system and a pair of protective glasses for pipe making just as with any other type of glassblowing. The ventilation system will help to eliminate the carbon dioxide buildup from the torch as well as levels of oxygen and prone that can build up when creating pipes, which can possibly result in an explosion.

How to Start on a Pipe

One important idea to keep in mind when creating pipes is that the process itself can be quite individual and eventually everyone tends to develop their own individual technique. The steps below will give you a good overview of the basic steps that should be taken to make a basic glass pipe.

The first step is to make sure you have your glass in a size that is manageable. Begin by using a tube of glass that is about 50mm thick and about 3 ½" long. You will need to gather the end up to about 6mm thickness. Remember that you will need to continually use the punty rod to attach and disattach as you work with the glass. Take the punty and hold it in the center and then use the torch flame to cut the tube. The mass should then be heated evenly until you have achieved the amount of molten glass you need. You can then begin blowing the bowl.

Keep in mind that when you blow into the blow tube you should inhale before you blow. If you inhale as you have the tube in your mouth it can cause you to inhale hot gases which can burn your lungs.

If the bowl appears to be lopsided it is most likely because some of the glass has been heated to a higher degree than the rest. If this happens, you will need to start over. Keep in mind that it is always much better to go ahead and start afresh at this point and ensure it is done right.

When adding designs into your pipe, you will need to use a flare. A flare can be created by opening a hole toward the end of the point. You can then maintain a reamer stationary inside the hole and hold the hole in the flame as you rotate the point until you achieve the desired flare. This may take some practice but when this technique is performed properly, the hole will automatically flare.

The next step is to blow the pipe while gathering glass toward the end. You can now draw any design you desire at this point. Another option would be to fume the pipe, which means covering the glass with a coating of metal oxide. The metal oxide is usually silver or gold to provide a decorative finish. To do this you will need to heat the pipe until it has almost become red hot. The coating will not adhere if it is not hot enough.

Another design style you might choose to use is known as inside out. This means that you do a coloring job by creating a point in the piece and then establishing a flare for access. After the color has been added you can close the flare.

Next you are going to heat the end of the cup and then immediately marver it down to the proper size for the blowtube. The cup and the blowtube will be attached using the white piece at the center. You will need to use a hot flame in order to blow out the end. Remember that gravity can be your friend at this point so allow it to work for you to condense the end.

Next, attach the punty to the center and heat the middle of your piece. When it has become soft enough, you can then start the second marvering in order to condense down the shape of the piece. Once this has been completed you will need to once again blow the pipe and turn it in order to create the desired size. Next, draw out the middle part and allow it to cool.

At this point you are almost nearing the finishing stage and you should be able to see how the finished piece will look. Next, you are going to reheat the part of the glass that is located near the blowtube and shape it. This will be done by hand. It takes some experience to do this, especially if you are trying to create more artistic shapes so try to be patient. You can now remove the punty and should then wipe down that part. Next, reheat the piece and then blow the end until it is rounded.

You will now be able to open a small hole by blowing into the blowtube. Heat the portion of the bowl where you would like to blow the hole, using a flame that is tightly focused, sometimes known as a needlepoint flame. You will need to blow hard in order to open up the hole in the side. Now, remove the glass and stop blowing to ensure the hole is not too big.

The next step is to create the bowl where the tobacco will be smoked. This is done by applying heat to the hole and pressing out the bowl using a carbon rod. A 5/8" carbon rod should be fine. Heat the area of the bowl where the hole is located and then press the carbon rod into the area you just heated. This will make a hollow. Make sure you keep the bottom portion of the bowl at a temperature that is lower in order to form a base that is stable.

After the bowl has the desired shape you will then apply a flame around the perimeter until it becomes red hot. You can then work on the pad and gently push it, but make sure you are continually turning it. After the pipe has been formed you will then be able to take off the blowtube and attach the punty once again. This will allow you to apply the finishing touches to the pipe.

After the punty has been removed for the last time, make sure you clean as well as smooth down the opening.

Keep in mind that glass pipes can be very fragile and if one should break there is really no way you can fix it.

Glossary

Amphora - A classic vase form, specifically with a waisted bottom.

Annealer - Refers to a large oven that is used to slowly cool glass from approximately 900F to room temperature in order to prevent the hot glass from developing cracks.

Annealing – Refers to the process of slow cooling heated glass through the annealing zone to prevent the presence of internal stress.

Annealing Point – Refers to the most efficient temperature at which to anneal a particular glass.

Annealing Zone – Refers to the temperature range beginning at the softening point and ending at the strain point. Typically between 1100°F and 600°F depending on the chemical makeup of the particular glass.

Avolio - Hourglass shaped connecting piece typically seen in Venetian style goblets. The avolio acts as a visual element, but also provides a thin spot that makes it easier to use the fork to load the goblet into the annealer.

Batch - Refers to the raw materials that are melted into glass. The process of melting batch is referred to as charging and is quite time-consuming.

Blank - Refers to a small hollow glass cylinder that is made using a specific color technique. Multiple blanks can be made from one large bubble and then each blank can be used to make a single piece.

Bent Glass - Refers to glass that has been heated in a kiln from room temperature to a temperature high enough to cause it to soften and sag into a mold. The finished item then will take the shape of the mold.

Block - Blocks are commonly made of cherry-wood and are used to shape, cool and center the glass. They are used early in the process of making a piece of glass, typically soon after the gather is made. There are special shaped blocks for making specific shaped work. Round blocks are used to make round paperweights and large marbles.

Burn Out – Refers to the process of pre-firing a mold or material in a vented kiln to remove, with heat, any unwanted contaminants.

Cane - Refers to the glass cylinder that consists of groups of rods of different colors that are bundled together and fused to form a design that is visible in cross section.

Catspaw - Refers to the surface texture that result from the chilling of hot glass on a cool table. The appearance is likened to the paw prints of a cat.

Color Bar - Most glass color come in the form of bar.

Compatibility – Refers to the absence of stress when different glasses are fused together. Glass that have the same or similar COE's are said to be compatible.

Core Drill - Refers to a water fed core-drill bit. Water feeds through the center of the bit and cools and then lubricates the bit as it cuts.

Crimp - There are many different crimps that are available for adding texture to glass.

Exact Torch - Refers to a standard high-pressure torch used in glassblowing to heat specific parts of a work-in-progress.

Fire Polish – Refers to the process of heating glass to the point where the surface has a glossy, wet appearance. A technique used to retain a shiny surface to glass after it has been ground or sand-blasted.

Flash Glass - A sheet of glass composed of a base layer with a thin contrasting layer of another color flashed or fused to the surface.

Frit - Small granules of glass ranging from fine powder to rock-salt size.

Frit Casting - A process in which a mold filled with frit is heated to the point where the frit fuses into a solid mass.

Full Fuse - Melting two or more pieces of glass into one single piece of glass. At full fuse the surface is without texture.

Gloryhole - Refers to a gas-fired furnace used to reheat work in progress; glass can only be manipulated when it is hot enough to be pliable. The doors on the gloryhole are opened to accommodate larger works.

Jacks - Refers to versatile tools used for shaping the glass, selectively cooling the glass and putting creases in the neck of vessels where they are to break for the transfer. Jacks are made in a variety of sizes and with different blade profiles for different types of work. Round jacks are used specifically for shaping avolios and other operations where a rounded contour is desirable.

Knock off table - Refers to a piece of hot shop equipment for making production-line work. It is usually covered with a woven silica fabric that can stand the heat of a new piece and will not wick enough heat. A piece can be knocked off onto the table, and then a torch can be used on the punty spot to soften any sharp edges before the piece is placed into the annealer.

Lamp Work – Refers to any glass working technique done using the direct flame of a torch.

Marver - Refers to a metal table used to shape, chill and center the piece.

Marvering at different angles is an essential skill for glassblowers to master.

Millefiori - Refers to glass objects made from masses of murrini slices.

Mold – Refers to any form made of a refractory material in which glass can be shaped by slumping into or over.

Murrini - Refers to a thin slice of complex glass cane that can be used as a component in another glass object.

Nugget - Refers to small irregularly shaped blobs of glass that are made by dropping a small amount of molten glass onto a flat surface. Also called globs.

Paddle - Refers to tools used to flatten the bottom of vessels. A metal paddle is necessary for sculpting solid glass into figures. Wooden paddles are also used as heatshields to protect the arms of the gaffer.

Pipe cooler - Refers to a tool that is used to spray water onto the pipe to cool it. It is imperative to keep the pipe turning when using the pipe cooler or the pipe could warp. Pipes should be cooled from the cool part first and then up towards the moil.

Pot Furnace - Refers to a melting chamber in which there is one or more ceramic pots. Batch is then fed into the individual pots through ports in the chamber walls, and when melted, glass is ladled from the pots through the same ports. The pot furnace makes it possible to melt several different glass colors at the same time, within a single melting chamber.

Rods - Refers to sticks of glass about the thickness of a pencil that are used commonly in glass bead making. They are available in many different colors.

Softening Point – Refers to the exact point at which unsupported glass, when heated, starts to soften and bend.

Stone - Small impurities in glass, such as a particle of furnace material.

Strain Point – Refers to the lowest annealing temperature. Location below the strain point any stress in glass is permanent.

Stress – Refers to a force creating tension and compression within glass that could cause unwanted breakage. Internal stress can be the result of poor annealing or fusing of incompatible glass.

Strike - When glass changes color during a heating cycle due to the oxidation atmosphere of the kiln.

Thermal Shock - Glass breakage caused by rapid or uneven heating or cooling.

Conclusion

I hope that you have enjoyed this introduction to glassblowing and that you have learned some of the critical concepts, techniques and procedures that will form the foundation for this beautiful craft. While the craft of glassblowing can take some time to master and should certainly be practiced with great care, with time and patience it is a craft that you can master, opening up the path for an enjoyable hobby or perhaps even a new business enterprise.

Where to Buy this Book

You can buy this book on Amazon. Just go to amazon.com (or your local Amazon site if available) and search for **"Learn How to Blow Glass by Anne Kramer"**.

You can also order it at any bookstore. Just give them the IBSN below:

ISBN 978-0-9866426-0-9

CPSIA information can be obtained at www.ICGtesting.com
Printed in the USA
LVOW010927301011

252644LV00003B/30/P

9 780986 642609